Copyright © 2023 by Marcus

All rights reserved. No part of this book may be reproduced or used in any manner without prior written permission from the copyright owner except for the use of quotations in a book review.

ISBN: 9798397181778

Imprint: Independently published

Disclaimer: All answers are correct as of March 27 2023.

Welcome to the
ICE HOCKEY
TRIVIA BOOK FOR ADULTS

CHECK OUT OUR BUMPER FOOTBALL, BASKETBALL, BASEBALL, & SOCCER TRIVIA BOOKS CONTAINING OVER 750 QUESTIONS FROM AN EXTRAORDINARY RANGE OF TOPICS ABOUT AMERICA'S MOST LOVED SPORTS. AVAILABLE NOW ON AMAZON.COM

CONTENTS PAGE

Warm-Up I	1
Warm-Up II	3
Round 1 - Founding & History	4
Round 2 - Stanley Cup	6
Round 3 - Trophy Names & History	8
Round 4 - Coaches	10
Round 5 - General Managers	12
Round 6 - Expansion & Relocation	14
Round 7 - Player Stats & Records	16
Round 8 - Wayne Gretzky	18
Round 9 - Mario Lemieux	20
Round 10 - First Overall Draft Picks I	22
Round 11 - Hockey TV & Movie Trivia	23
Round 12 - Rule Changes	25
Round 13 - NHL Points Leaders	27
Round 14 - Mascots	28
Round 15 - First Overall Draft Picks II	30
Round 16 - NHL Draft Steals	31
Round 17 - Anaheim Ducks	34
Round 18 - Arizona Coyotes	35
Round 19 - Boston Bruins	36
Round 20 - Buffalo Sabres	37
Round 21 - Calgary Flames	38
Round 22 - Carolina Hurricanes	39
Round 23 - Chicago Blackhawks	40
Round 24 - Colorado Avalanche	41
Round 25 - Columbus Blue Jackets	42
Round 26 - Dallas Stars	43
Round 27 - Detroit Red Wings	44
Round 28 - Edmonton Oilers	45
Round 29 - Florida Panthers	46
Round 30 - Los Angeles Kings	47
Round 31 - Minnesota Wild	48
Round 32 - Montreal Canadiens	49
Round 33 - Nashville Predators	50
Round 34 - New Jersey Devils	51
Round 35 - New York Islanders	52
Round 36 - New York Rangers	53
Round 37 - Ottawa Senators	54
Round 38 - Philadelphia Flyers	55
Round 39 - Pittsburgh Penguins	56
Round 40 - San Jose Sharks	57
Round 41 - Seattle Kraken	58
Round 42 - St. Louis Blues	59
Round 43 - Tampa Bay Lightning	60
Round 44 - Toronto Maple Leafs	61
Round 45 - Vancouver Canucks	62
Round 46 - Vegas Golden Knights	63
Round 47 - Washington Capitals	64
Round 48 - Winnipeg Jets	65
Round 49 - Stanley Cup Match Ups	66
Round 50 - Opening Night & NHL Debuts	67
Round 51 - Drafts of Famous Players	69
Round 52 - Olympic & World Cup Teams	71
Round 53 - Minor League	73
Round 54 - Hall of Fame	75
Round 55 - NHL Draft Firsts	77
Round 56 - NCAA Hockey	78
Round 57 - Arenas I	79
Round 58 - Arenas II	80

WARM-UP 1

Some nice easy questions to get you warmed up!

1. In what city would you find the Senators?

2. How many different positions are on a hockey team?

3. How many goalies does a normal team carry on their roster?

4. How many divisions are in the NHL?

5. What is the primary developmental league for the NHL?

6. What is the premier double AA hockey league for the NHL?

7. What is the name of the primary league that NHL clubs draft from?

8. Can you name all three of the leagues that make up the league the NHL primarily drafts from?

9. What former NHL player is referred to as "The Great One"?

10. What NHL player is and or was referred to as "The Next One"?

11) What former NHL player is referred to as "Mr. Hockey"?

12) What NHL team refers to their home city as "Hockey Town"?

13) What U.S. state is often called "The State of Hockey"?

14) What is the most popular beverage sold at NHL games?

15) What are the ingredients for poutine?

16) In what movie was the quote "If we play them ten times, they might win nine. But not this game. Not tonight" said?

17) How many pucks are used during a typical NHL game?

18) What does the NHL do with pucks before they can be used in a game?

19) What are NHL pucks made from?

20) When did hockey goalies start wearing masks?

WARM-UP II

Final warm-up round. Can you name all 32 NHL teams by division? Bonus points if you can put them in order of their 2022 regular season standings.

Atlantic	Central

Metropolitan	Pacific

ROUND 1 — FOUNDING & HISTORY

1. What year was the NHL founded? 1918, 1920, 1919, 1917

2. What league preceded the NHL?

3. What was the first NHL team in the United States?

4. What were the "original six" teams?

5. What team is considered the seventh "original six" team?

6. What NHL team played in Montreal from 1924-1938 (not the Canadiens)?

7. Who is the Vezina Trophy named after?

8. What was the second team that played in New York from 1925-1941?

9. What was the hockey team that played in Toronto from 1919-1927?

10. What were the two leagues that competed with the NHL for players and the Stanley Cup?

11. What was the name of the first NHL team in Pennsylvania?

12. What was the name of the first NHL team in Philadelphia?

13. Who was the first NHL player to score 50 goals in a season?

14. Who were the first teams to play for the Stanley Cup? Who won?

15. What was the highest-scoring game in NHL history?

16. Who is considered the first NHL superstar?

17. What major world event caused the NHL to shrink down to six teams?

18. What part of the Canadian military were the members of the Toronto 228th Battalion a part of?

19. Where was the first meeting held between representatives of the NHL teams?

20. Who was the first goalie to score a goal in NHL History?

ROUND 2: STANLEY CUP

1. Who donated the Stanley Cup to the NHA/NHL?

2. What was the original name of the Stanley Cup?

3. When was the first Stanley Cup awarded?

4. What was the first American team to win the Stanley Cup?

5. What team has won the most Stanley Cups?

6. Who is the only goalie to appear on the Stanley Cup as a captain of a Cup-winning team?

7. Who was the first player to win the Stanley Cup and an Olympic Gold Medal?

8. How many Stanley Cups did the New York Islanders and Edmonton Oilers win combined between 1980 and 1990?

9. Which year was there not a Stanley Cup Awarded because of the influenza pandemic?

10. What team made the Stanley Cup in 1968, 1969, and 1970 and not only lost all three but were swept?

11. What NHL player holds the record for the most career goals in the Stanley Cup Finals?

12. How was Boston spelled on the Stanley Cup after their 1972 win?

13. How was Adam Deadmarsh's name spelled on the Cup after Colorado's 1996 win?

14. What Dallas Star allegedly tossed the Stanley Cup from a second story into a pool and missed?

15. How much does the Stanley Cup weigh?

16. Who was the first NHL player to take the Stanley Cup on its first European Trip?

17. What Stanley Cup winner had his child baptized in the Stanley Cup in 1996?

18. How many days a year does the Stanley Cup travel?

19. True or False: In 1924 the Montreal Canadiens left the Stanley Cup on the side of the road.

20. What NHL player has had his name on the Stanley Cup the most at 11 times?

ROUND 3: TROPHY NAMES & HISTORY

1. Who was the Prince of Wales Trophy named after?

2. Who was Clarence S. Campbell?

3. What year did the NHL introduce the Presidents' Trophy?

4. Who votes for the winner of the Hart Memorial Trophy?

5. What is the factor that determines who wins the Lady Byng Memorial Trophy?

6. Who votes on who wins the Vezina Trophy?

7. Who is the Calder Memorial Trophy named after?

8. What NHL organization has won the most Art Ross Trophies?

9. What former NHL player has won the James Norris Memorial Trophy 8 times?

10. What goalie has won the Conn Smythe Trophy three times?

11. What unfortunate record does Bill Masterton hold, the reason the trophy is named after him?

12. What governing body votes for the winner of the Ted Lindsay Award?

13. To what member of an NHL organization is the Jack Adams Award awarded too?

14. Who was Frank J. Selke?

15. What two former NHL goalies are tied at 5 each for William M. Jennings Trophies?

16. What is the characteristic of a player that makes them eligible for consideration for the King Clancy Memorial Trophy?

17. What stat must players lead in to win the Maurice "Rocket" Richard Trophy?

18. Who awards the Mark Messier Leadership Award to the winner every season?

19. In what year was the General Manager of the Year Award renamed and why?

20. Who is the E.J. McGuire Award of Excellence awarded to?

ROUND 4: COACHES

1. What NHL coach has won the most games in NHL history?

2. How many Stanley Cups did Scotty Bowman win in his career?

3. Who was the first Colorado Avalanche coach to win the Jack Adams?

4. Who was the youngest head coach to win the Stanley Cup?

5. Who is the only person in NHL history to win the Stanley Cup as a player, coach, and general manager?

6. Who was the head coach of the Philadelphia Flyers during their back-to-back Cup victories?

7. Who coached the New York Islanders to 4 straight Stanley Cup victories?

8. What NHL team did Wayne Gretzky briefly coach?

9. What NHL coach has won the most Jack Adams Awards at 3?

10. Who is the only NHL coach to win the Jack Adams Award back-to-back?

11 What NHL coach turned down going to law school to coach the Philadelphia Flyers?

12 What Red Wings coach was the worst in team history?

13 What was the first NHL team Herb Brooks coached?

14 What was the numerical value of New York Rangers coach John Tortorella's fine after the 2012 Winter Classic?

15 Why was Vancouver Canucks head coach Harry Neale suspended for 10 games in 1982?

16 What NHL coach would routinely find loopholes in the NHL rulebook and is credited with being the first coach to pull the goalie?

17 Who is the longest-tenured coach of all-time in the NHL?

18 Which coach has the second-highest number of games coached in the NHL with over 1,800 matches?

19 Who was the first head coach of the Vegas Golden Knights?

20 Who was the first head coach of the Seattle Kraken?

ROUND 5 — GENERAL MANAGERS

1. Who is the longest-serving general manager in NHL history?

2. Who was appointed as the Winnipeg Jets general manager in 2011?

3. Who was the first general manager of the Vegas Golden Knights?

4. Who was the first general manager of the Seattle Kraken?

5. Who was the general manager that took over the New Jersey Devils in 1987 and won the Stanley Cup with them in 1995?

6. Who was the general manager of the New York Islanders from 2006 to 2018?

7. Who was the general manager that led the Colorado Avalanche to 2 Stanley Cups, 2 Presidents' Cups, 2 conference titles, and 11 division titles?

8. What Red Wings general manager won the Stanley Cup 7 times from 1936 to 1955?

9. What Red Wings general manager started the 25 straight consecutive playoff appearances?

10. What was the name of the general manager that brought Wayne Gretzky to Edmonton?

11. What was the name of the Montreal Canadiens general manager who made the trade for Guy Lafleur?

12. Who was the first general manager to be from Europe?

13. Who became an NHL general manager in 2016 after 26 seasons as head coach of the Brandon Wheat Kings?

14. Who was the youngest general manager in NHL history?

15. Which man played for the New York Rangers and Islanders and has been general manager of the Islanders, Coyotes and Flames?

16. What is the name of the NHL general manager who won the most Stanley Cups?

17. What New York Islanders general manager traded Zdeno Chara and Roberto Luongo and is considered one of the worst general managers in NHL and Islanders team history?

18. What is the name of the general manager whose failure arguably moved the Thrashers out of Atlanta?

19. What was the name of the Calgary Flames general manager who cut Martin St. Louis, who then went on to beat the Flames in the Stanley Cup with Tampa Bay?

20. What is the name of the Flyers general manager who arguably traded 2 Stanley Cups to the Quebec Nordiques for Eric Lindors?

ROUND 6
EXPANSION & RELOCATION

1. What was the name of the 4 World Hockey Association teams that were folded into the NHL during the 1979 WHA-NHL merger?

2. What was the name and city of the team that the Arizona Coyotes relocated from in 1996?

3. What was the name of the city and team that the Carolina Hurricanes relocated from in 1997?

4. Name two of the 6 teams the NHL added in the 1967 expansion?

5. What was the name of the first NHL team in Denver, Colorado?

6. What 2 NHL teams were added in 1970?

7. What two cities did the New Jersey Devils call home before New Jersey?

8. What are the names of the only 2 NHL teams to call Ohio home?

9. Where did the Minnesota North Stars relocate to after the 1993 season?

10. What team was added to the NHL in 1998?

11. What two teams entered the NHL in 2000?

12. What was the last team in not just the NHL, but in the top 4 major North American sports to cease operations 1978?

13. What team was the most successful expansion team in NHL history during their first season?

14. What expansion team had the worst first season in NHL history?

15. Who was the first player signed by the Vegas Golden Knights?

16. What is the only NHL team that currently plays that was once two separate franchises?

17. Who scored the first goal in Vegas Golden Knight's history?

18. What was the name of the NHL team that almost joined the NHL in 1997 in Norfolk, Virginia?

19. Where were the Pittsburgh Penguins rumored to move to when arena negotiations soured?

20. What city did the Calgary Flames move from? The team is still honored by the assistant captain's jersey letter.

ROUND 7
PLAYER STATS & RECORDS

1. Who is the all-time NHL leader in the regular season games played?

2. Who is the all-time NHL leader in points scored?

3. Who is the all-time NHL leader in assists?

4. Who is second place for all-time NHL points scored?

5. Who is the leader in penalty minutes accrued in NHL history?

6. Who is the all-time leader in plus-minus?

7. What two cities did the New Jersey Devils call home before New Jersey?

8. Who holds the record for the longest suspension in NHL history?

9. What two players are tied for the most seasons played in the NHL?

10. What NHL player has the most games played including playoffs?

11. How old was Gordie Howe when he played in his last NHL game?

12. How many Stanley Cups did Henri Richard win? Leads the NHL in Cup wins.

13. What player holds the record for most goals scored in their first NHL game?

14. What NHL legend holds the record for most goals scored in different ways?

15. Who scored the most goals in an expansion team's inaugural season?

16. What former NHL player leads defensemen in points scored?

17. Who is the most recent NHL goalie to score a goal?

18. What NHL goalie holds the most penalty minutes in a single season?

19. What player holds the record for most NHL teams played for at 12 teams?

20. What former Flyer holds the most penalty minutes in one season?

ROUND 8

WAYNE GRETZKY

1. What WHA team signed Gretzky to his first professional contract in 1978?

2. Where was Wayne Gretzky when he found out he was being moved from Indianapolis to Edmonton during the final WHA season?

3. Did Gretzky win an Avco World Trophy?

4. What two teams did Gretzky play for in the OMJHL, now the OHL, that are still around today?

5. How many points did Gretzky record in his highest point-totaling season?

6. What four NHL teams did Gretzky play for?

7. Did Wayne Gretzky ever win gold at the Olympics as a player?

8. How many Canada Cup Gold medals did Gretzky win?

9. How many Stanley Cups did Gretzky win?

10. What did the Edmonton Oilers get in return when they traded Gretzky to Los Angeles?

11. Why did Gretzky wear #99 instead of #9?

12. How many times was Gretzky traded?

13. How many Hart Trophies did Gretzky win consecutively?

14. How long did it take Gretzky to score 50 goals in the 1981-1982 season?

15. How many records does Gretzky own and share?

16. What newspaper caused a stir in 1982 when they said Wayne Gretzky was coming to the Toronto Maple Leafs on April 1st?

17. How many points did Gretzky score in his rookie season?

18. What year did Wayne Gretzky retire?

19. How many seasons did Gretzky coach the Phoenix Coyotes?

20. Name one of the two enforcers Gretzky had during his career.

ROUND 9: MARIO LEMIEUX

1. What was the name of the QMJHL team that Mario played for?

2. What year was Lemieux drafted first overall?

3. How many combined games did Lemieux play for the Pittsburgh Penguins?

4. How many all-star games did Mario participate in?

5. How many Stanley Cups did Lemieux win as a player?

6. How many Stanley Cups did Lemieux win as a general manager?

7. What team did Mario play for when he returned from cancer treatment with the fans giving him a standing ovation?

8. True or False: Lemieux was the first player and owner to win a Stanley Cup?

9. What year did Lemieux buy the Pittsburgh Penguins and why?

10. What current Pittsburgh Penguin lived with Mario Lemieux at the beginning of his career?

11. True or False: He is the first professional athlete to own the team he played for.

12. How many 5 goal games did Mario have?

13. How many games was Mario's longest goal streak?

14. How many short-handed goals did he score in the NHL regular season? 39, 49, 59 or 69?

15. Why did Lemieux wear #66?

16. True or False: He is the only player to score 70+ powerplay points in a single season? False?

17. True or False: His highest point total in a single season was 200.

18. Name all 5 ways Lemieux scored a goal in his famous 5-goal game.

19. In which Olympics did Lemieux win his only Gold Medal?

20. Name one of Mario Lemieux's three nicknames?

ROUND 10: FIRST OVERALL DRAFT PICKS I

Write the name of the first overall draft pick based on the team and year they were drafted for.

Year	Team	Player
2003	Pittsburgh Penguins	
2004	Washington Capitals	
2005	Pittsburgh Penguins	
2006	St. Louis Blues	
2007	Chicago Blackhawks	
2008	Tampa Bay Lightning	
2009	New York Islanders	
2010	Edmonton Oilers	
2011	Edmonton Oilers	
2012	Edmonton Oilers	
2013	Colorado Avalanche	
2014	Florida Panthers	
2015	Edmonton Oilers	
2016	Toronto Maple Leafs	
2017	New Jersey Devils	
2018	Buffalo Sabres	
2019	New Jersey Devils	
2020	New York Rangers	
2021	Buffalo Sabres	
2022	Montreal Canadiens	

ROUND 11: HOCKEY TV & MOVIE TRIVIA

1. Who played Herb Brooks in the movie Miracle?

2. What real life hockey player was the movie Goon based off?

3. What NHL player made a cameo in The Mighty Ducks?

4. What current Dallas Stars player made a cameo in Goon 2: Last of the Enforcers?

5. What NHL team did the fictional Mystery Eskimos team play in the 1999 film Mystery, Alaska?

6. What actor played player-coach Reggie Dunlop in the 1977 movie Slapshot?

7. What were the numbers for the three Hanson brothers in Slapshot?

8. Which actor who played a Hanson brother played in the NHL?

9. What current NHL goalie recreated Yvon Barrettes legendary opening scene from Slapshot?

10. What former NHL tough guy did Doug Glatt fight in Goon?

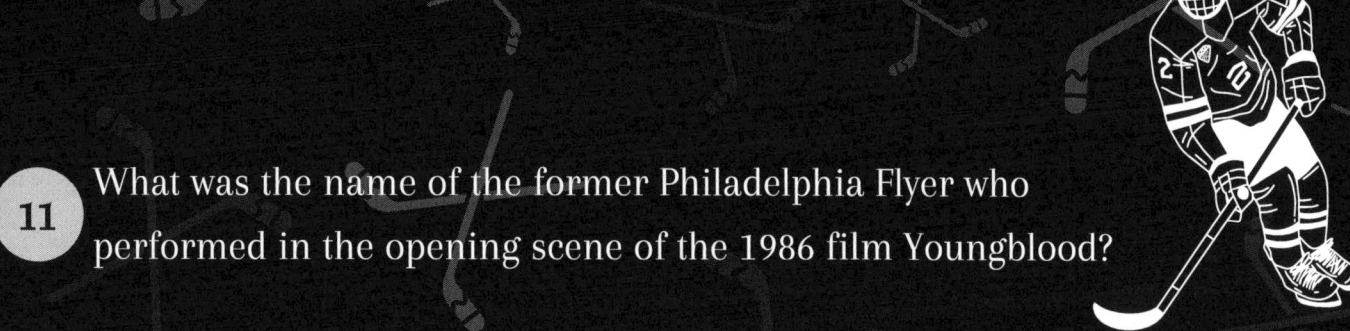

11. What was the name of the former Philadelphia Flyer who performed in the opening scene of the 1986 film Youngblood?

12. Which one of the Matrix stars played goalie and decided to act over pursuing a career in professional hockey?

13. Not so much a hockey movie but more of a documentary, what Stanley Cup champion played for the Danbury Trashers during the 2004-05 lockout?

14. What Goon 2: Last of the Enforcers star played professional hockey in the Netherlands allowing 5.62 GAA a game?

15. What is the name of the team that plays in Letterkenny, Ontario in the TV show Letterkenny?

16. What is the name of the Kent County team in Letterkenny?

17. What NHL team are both the Orange Town Assassins and Halifax Highlanders logos/ uniforms based from?

18. What was the name of the company that sponsored the Mighty Ducks at the Junior Goodwill Games?

19. Who is the Minnesota Miracle Man?

20. What Canadian television show did Nathan MacKinnon appear as himself in 2017?

ROUND 12: RULE CHANGES

1. What rule is Roger Neilson best remembered for creating?

2. What did Sean Avery do to create the Sean Avery rule and what is the rule?

3. Bill Durnan was captain of the Canadiens during the 1947-48 season. Why did the NHL make a rule that goalies could not be captains?

4. What goalie was made team captain of the Vancouver Canucks in the 2008-09 season after the team received an exception from the previously mentioned rule?

5. What former Philadelphia Flyer was the reason for introducing the diving penalty call?

6. What former Chicago Blackhawks goalie constantly crossed center ice with the puck leading to the NHL introducing the rule that they could no longer do so?

7. What is the Wayne Gretzky/ Edmonton Oilers rule?

8. What is the Banana Blade Curve rule?

9. Why was the 'Skate in crease rule' abolished?

10. What NHL player was the reason the Calder Cup has an age limit?

11) What is the Rob Ray rule?

12) What is the Matt Cooke rule?

13) What is the Reijo Ruotsalaninen rule?

14) What goalie boldly sewed a web in between his legs?

15) What New Jersey Devils legend caused the goalie trapezoid rule?

16) What Detroit Red Wings legend caused the elbowing and kneeing rules?

17) What NHL team was so prolific on the powerplay in the 50's the NHL had to change minor penalty rules so that a player could leave the box after a power play goal was scored?

18) What Canadiens goalie helped create the goalie helmet rule after he broke his nose during a game?

19) What current NHL player forced NHL officials to re-evaluate the slashing penalty after they slashed a player's finger clean off?

20) What player went blatantly offsides and scored on a breakaway goal, allowing the Colorado Avalanche to win the game 6-5? This goal allowed for the coaches' challenge.

ROUND 13: NHL POINTS LEADERS

How well do you know the top 20 NHL points leaders? There is a point for getting their name and a point for naming one of the teams they played for in their NHL career, good luck!

Rank	Team(s)	GP	Points	Player
1	EDM, LAK, STL, NYR	1,514	2,857	
2	PIT, WSH, NYR, PHI, DAL, BOS, NJD, FLA, CGY	1,733	1,921	
3	EDM, NYR, VAN	1,756	1,887	
4	DET, HFD	1,767	1,850	
5	HFD, PIT, CAR, TOR	1,731	1,798	
6	DET, LAK, NYR	1,348	1,771	
7	DET	1,514	1,755	
8	PIT	915	1,723	
9	QUE, COL	1,378	1,641	
10	CHI, BOS, NYR	1,282	1,590	
11	BOS, COL	1,612	1,579	
12	BOS, SJS, TOR, FLA	1,714	1,539	
13	PIT, PHI, MTL, CAR, ATL, TBL, BOS	1,652	1,533	
14	EDM, PIT, LAK, DET, HFD, PHI, CHI, CAR, BOS	1,409	1,531	
15	PIT	1,185	1,497	
16	WSH	1,345	1,483	
17	CHI	1,396	1,467	
18	WIN, ANA, SJS, COL	1,451	1,457	
19	NYI, PIT	1,279	1,425	
20	DET, STL, BOS, WSH, PHI, ANA, EDM	1,337	1,420	

ROUND 14: MASCOTS

1. What is the only NHL team that has a non-costumed mascot?

2. What are the three NHL teams that don't have a mascot?

3. What NHL team has never had a mascot?

4. What is the name of the Philadelphia Flyers mascot?

5. What type of dog is the Colorado Avalanche's mascot?

6. Why is the Los Angeles Kings mascot Bailey's number 72?

7. Why is the Red Wings Mascot an Octopus?

8. What type of animal is the Boston Bruins mascot?

9. Why is the Leafs' mascot named Carlton, and why is his #60?

10. What type of reptile is the Vegas Golden Knights mascot Chance?

11. Who was the Flyers' mascot before Gritty?

12. What type of dog is the Calgary Flames mascot Harvey the Hound?

13. Why is Howler the Arizona Coyotes mascot number 96?

14. What type of whale is Fin the Whale in Vancouver?

15. For what team is Hunter a mascot, and what type of cat is he?

16. Which NHL team's mascot is almost identical to their AHL team's mascot? (Hint: both teams have the same name and play in the same state)

17. What are the names of the Jets' mascots?

18. What is the number that Minnesota Wild mascot Nordy wears on his jersey?

19. What are the names of both mascots for the Florida Panthers?

20. What is the name of the Canadiens mascot, and which former MLB team was he a mascot for?

ROUND 15
FIRST OVERALL DRAFT PICKS II

Same as Round 10 but this time for the first overall draft picks from 1983-2002.

Year	Team	Player
1983	Minnesota North Stars	
1984	Pittsburgh Penguins	
1985	Toronto Maple Leafs	
1986	Detroit Red Wings	
1987	Buffalo Sabres	
1988	Minnesota North Stars	
1989	Quebec Nordiques	
1990	Quebec Nordiques	
1991	Quebec Nordiques	
1992	Tampa Bay Lightning	
1993	Ottawa Senators	
1994	Florida Panthers	
1995	Ottawa Senators	
1996	Ottawa Senators	
1997	Boston Bruins	
1998	Tampa Bay Lightning	
1999	Atlanta Thrashers	
2000	New York Islanders	
2001	Atlanta Thrashers	
2002	Columbus Blue Jackets	

ROUND 16: NHL DRAFT STEALS

1. Who did the Minnesota Wild take in the 5th round of the 2015 NHL Entry Draft 135th overall?

2. Who was the player that the Tampa Bay Lightning took in the 3rd round of the 2014 NHL Entry Draft 79th overall?

3. Who was the player that the Chicago Blackhawks selected in the second round of the 2016 NHL draft 39th overall? Possibly the greatest draft steal in the last 5 years.

4. In 2015, the Pittsburgh Penguins first round pick went to the Edmonton Oilers via a trade, and then later the Edmonton Oilers traded that pick to the New York Islanders. Who did the Islanders pick 16th overall in the 2015 NHL draft?

5. Who did the Montreal Canadiens select in the 2010 NHL Entry Draft 147th overall?

6. Who did the Nashville Predators select 112th overall in the 2014 NHL Entry Draft?

7. What New Jersey native did the Calgary Flames steal during the 2011 NHL Entry Draft 104th overall?

8 This 6-time Vezina Trophy-winning goalie wasn't selected until the 10th round (there were only 21 teams) of the 1983 NHL Entry Draft and was selected 199th overall by the Chicago Blackhawks, who was it?

9 This former Detroit Red Wings assistant captain wasn't selected until the 6th round of the 1998 NHL Entry Draft and won two Stanley Cups with the team, who was it?

10 What Blueshirts legendary goaltender was selected 204 spots after Rick DiPietro in the 2000 NHL Entry Draft? He went on to win 5 Vezina Trophies during his career.

11 This former Red Wings captain may have been the forward steal of the 2000 NHL Entry Draft. What player did the Red Wings take 210th overall in that draft?

12 This 3rd round pick was the talk of the show during the 1980s winning multiple Cups with Wayne Gretzky. Who did the Edmonton Oilers take in the 3rd round of the 1979 NHL Entry Draft 48th overall?

13 Yet another Red Wings captain was plucked out of the first round. Who did the Red Wings take 53rd overall in the 1989 NHL Entry Draft?

14 The San Jose Sharks took this Finnish goaltending legend in the 5th round in the 1995 NHL Draft. He only played two seasons there before being traded to Calgary, who was this goalie?

15 The Boston Bruins had three consecutive 1st round picks in the 2015 NHL Entry Draft, all but one of those 3 picks have been NHL regulars, who was the player taken after those 3 picks?

16 In the 1980 NHL Entry Draft, the Edmonton Oilers had quite the draft, they got Paul Coffey 6th overall. What right wing legend was taken in the 4th round 69th overall by the Edmonton Oilers in the same draft?

17 In the 1998 NHL Entry Draft, the Tampa Bay Lightning took Vincent Lecavalier 1st overall. In the 3rd round of that same draft, the Lightning took their 6th overall points scorer in team history, who was it?

18 The Dallas Stars got quite the player in the 129th overall in the 2007 NHL Entry Draft. He is considered one of the NHL's best all-round players, who was it?

19 This player was drafted by the Sharks in the 7th round of the 2003 Entry Draft, he is often referred to as Captain America, who was he?

20 These two NHL goalies were both drafted in the same round of the 2003 NHL Entry draft in the 9th round. One was taken 271st overall by the Montreal Canadiens, the other 291st overall by the Ottawa Senators. The two were teammates in St. Louis and are the first teammates to record six or more shutouts in one season. Who were there?

ROUND 17 — ANAHEIM DUCKS

1. Who was the first team captain in Anaheim Ducks history?

2. Did Bobby Ryan win a Cup in 2007 with the Anaheim Ducks?

3. What number did Jean-Sebastian Giguere wear?

4. What team did the Anaheim Ducks defeat in the 2007 Stanley Cup Final?

5. Who leads the Anaheim Ducks in games played?

6. What year were the Ducks founded?

7. What was the name of the AHL team the Ducks owners bought and moved to San Diego?

8. Who are the three players whose numbers were retired by the Duck

9. Who was the Ducks' captain from 1996-2003?

10. Who leads the Ducks in franchise playoff points?

ROUND 18: ARIZONA COYOTES

1. Who was the first goaltender to get 40 wins in a season for the Yotes?

2. Who was the first player in franchise history to score 75 goals?

3. Whose number is the only number retired by the Arizona Coyotes and what is the number?

4. The Arizona Coyotes have had 4 captains, name two.

5. Who was the first player in franchise history to win NHL rookie of the year?

6. Who are the Coyotes' AHL affiliate?

7. What is the only season trophy the Arizona Coyotes have?

8. Who is the only player whose number has been retired by the Coyotes?

9. What team did Shane Doan almost sign with in free agency? Potentially ending his career-long tenure with the Coyotes.

10. Who did the Arizona Coyotes draft in the 2013 Entry Draft 12th overall?

ROUND 19: BOSTON BRUINS

1. What year were the Boston Bruins founded?

2. In what years Stanley Cup did Bobby Orr famously fly through the air clinching the series and who did they defeat?

3. Why did Ray Bourque change is number from #7 to #77?

4. The Boston Bruins were the first team to break the color barrier. What was the name of the player on their team?

5. Who were the three players that made up the "700 Pound Line"?

6. How many numbers have the Bruins retired?

7. Who holds the franchise record for most goals in one season?

8. Who leads the Bruins in all-time points?

9. What is the name of the Bruins AHL affiliate?

10. What year was Brad Marchand drafted?

ROUND 20: BUFFALO SABRES

1. Who were the three players that made up the "French Connection Line"?

2. What Buffalo Sabres general manager drafted Taro Tsujumoto, a player who did not exist, 183rd overall in the 1974 NHL Amateur Draft?

3. What is the name of the goalie who had his carotid artery severed in a game against the St. Louis Blues?

4. What was Danny Briere's nickname during his time in Buffalo?

5. Who was the first Buffalo Sabres goalie to achieve 40 wins in one season?

6. Who owns the Buffalo Sabres?

7. How many Stanley Cups have the Bruins won?

8. Whose #39 jersey was retired by the Sabres in 2015?

9. When was the last time the Sabres won a President's Trophy?

10. Who was the 13th captain in the Sabres' history?

3. Who was the first player in Calgary Flames history to lead the league in goals and points?

4. What is the name of the Calgary Flames player who won the NHL Rookie of the Year award at the of 31?

5. What was Kent Nilsson's nickname?

6. What was "Blasty"?

7. Who was the Flames' captain from 2013-2021?

8. Whose jersey was retired by the Flames in 2019?

9. Who is the second all-time points scorer in the Flames' history?

10. How many Stanley Cups have the Flames won?

ROUND 22: CAROLINA HURRICANES

1. Who was the first Carolina Hurricane to win Rookie of the Year?

2. Who did the Carolina Hurricanes defeat in the 2006 Stanley Cup Finals to win their only Cup so far?

3. What is the name that the 2018-2019 Carolina Hurricanes received from Don Cherry on Hockey Night in Canada?

4. Who was the first emergency goalie in NHL history to win a game and what team did he beat with the Carolina Hurricanes?

5. What former Hurricane scored the "Miracle at Molson" in 2002?

6. When did the Hurricanes win their first Stanley Cup?

7. Whose #17 was retired by the Flames in 2011?

8. How many NHL teams did Brind'Amor play for and who were they?

9. Who was the Hurricanes' captain from 2010-2016?

10. Who leads the Hurricanes franchise in goals scored?

ROUND 23
CHICAGO BLACKHAWKS

1. In 2007, Jonathan Toews faced off against his childhood idol and won the faceoff against them. Who was the player Jonathan Toews idolized as a kid?

2. The last of the 'Original Six' to do so, when did the Chicago Blackhawks win their first Stanley Cup?

3. Who was the first player to have their number retired by the Chicago Blackhawks and how many seasons did he play for them?

4. Who has the most penalty minutes in Chicago Blackhawks franchise history?

5. What was Bobby Hull's nickname while playing in Chicago?

6. What Blackhawks player rapped at one of their Stanley Cup Parades?

7. What were the Blackhawks named after?

8. What was the Blackhawks' goal song during the 2009-2010 playoff run?

9. Who leads the Blackhawks in franchise playoff points?

10. What AHL team did Patrick Sharp win the Calder Cup with?

ROUND 24
COLORADO AVALANCHE

1. What Avalanche player broke Kris Drapers jaw in Game 6 of the 1996 Western Conference Finals?

2. How many consecutive division titles did the franchise win combined with Colorado and Quebec?

3. Between the Colorado Avalanche and Quebec Nordiques, the team has had 6 Calder Memorial Trophy winners, who were they?

4. Who is the only Avalanche player to win the Maurice "Rocket" Richard Trophy?

5. What teams did the Avalanche beat in their first two Stanley Cup victories?

6. What was the name of the Avalanche's arena before the name change to Ball Arena?

7. What was Joe Sakic's number before changing to #19?

8. What was the score when they won their third Stanley Cup against the Lightning in 2022?

9. What is the name of the line that consists of Gabriel Landeskog, Mikko Rantanen and Nathan MacKinnon?

10. Who is second in Avalanche's all-time points scoring?

ROUND 25
COLUMBUS BLUE JACKETS

1. Who was the first Columbus Blue Jackets' player to score 80 points in one season?

2. What is the longest winning streak in Columbus Blue Jackets franchise history?

3. In what round of the NHL Entry Draft was Cam Atkinson selected?

4. Who was the first Blue Jacket to win Rookie of the year, doing so in 2009?

5. What team did the Blue Jackets blow out in 2016 10-0?

6. Who did the Blue Jackets sweep in the 2018-2019 playoffs?

7. Who is the only Blue Jackets goalie to win a Vezina Trophy?

8. Who owns the title of franchise scoring leader for the Blue Jackets?

9. What historical event inspired the Blue Jackets' name and jersey design?

10. Who was the first captain in Blue Jackets' history?

ROUND 26
DALLAS STARS

1. What year did the North Stars relocate to Dallas?

2. What former player leads the Dallas Stars all-time in points?

3. Who did the Dallas Stars defeat to win their first Stanley Cup championship?

4. Who was the first Dallas Star to win the Conn Smythe Trophy in 1999?

5. What goalie leads the Dallas Stars in wins?

6. Whose jersey was most recently retired by the Stars?

7. Who leads the Stars in assists in one season?

8. Who did the Stars draft 10th overall in 2013?

9. Who was the other team Mike Modano played for besides either of the Stars?

10. Who is the Stars' only Selke Trophy winner?

ROUND 27: DETROIT RED WINGS

1. Name one of the two names the Detroit Red Wings were known as before 1932.

2. Who was the longest-serving captain in Detroit Red Wings history?

3. Who were the "Bruise Brothers"?

4. Between 1984 and 2016, how many times did the Detroit Red Wings make the playoffs?

5. What team did the Detroit Red Wings brawl on "Bloody Wednesday"?

6. Name two of Detroit's "Russian Five"?

7. Whose number was retired in 2014?

8. How many division championships have the Red Wings won?

9. Where did the Red Wings play before the Joe Louis Arena?

10. Who owned the Red Wings from 1982 till his death in 2017?

ROUND 28
EDMONTON OILERS

1. Who was the Edmonton Oilers first ever NHL Entry Draft selection?

2. What is the name of the Edmonton Oilers player who scored 8 points, 4 goals and 4 assists, versus the Chicago Blackhawks in 2012?

3. What was the name of the Edmonton Oilers owner who traded Gretzky?

4. What were the Edmonton Oilers known as during the 1972-1973 WHA season?

5. Who was the captain of the Edmonton Oilers before Connor McDavid?

6. Who did the Oilers draft 3rd overall in the 2014 Draft?

7. Who has the most penalty minutes in one season for the Oilers?

8. Who do the Oilers face in the 'Battle of Alberta'?

9. How many numbers have the Oilers retired?

10. Where did the Oilers play before Rogers Place?

ROUND 29
FLORIDA PANTHERS

1. What year were the Florida Panthers founded?

2. Who was the Panthers' first general manager in team history?

3. What was the longest shootout in Florida Panthers' history? Bonus: Who scored the winner?

4. What did Panthers fans throw onto the ice during the 1995-1996 season?

5. Who was the Panthers' first Rookie of the Year?

6. What city do the Panthers play in?

7. What flag is on the Panthers' Uniform?

8. Who was the Panthers' first Selke Trophy Winner?

9. What Panthers goalie won Gold at the World Juniors in 2021?

10. Whose number did the Panthers retire in 2020?

ROUND 30: LOS ANGELES KINGS

1. Who were the players that made up "The Triple Crown Line"?

2. What two Metropolitan Division teams did the Los Angeles Kings beat to win their 2 Stanley Cups?

3. Who was the Kings' first pick in the 1967 expansion draft?

4. Who was the first goalie in Kings' history to get 10 shutouts in one season?

5. Who did the Kings pick with the 11th overall pick in the 2005 NHL Entry Draft?

6. Who was the Kings' captain before Anze Kopitar?

7. Who did the Kings beat after being down 3-0 in a playoff series in 2014?

8. Who was the head coach of the Kings for their 2 Cups?

9. Who leads the Kings in all-time points?

10. True or False: Wayne Gretzky won a Cup with the Kings.

ROUND 31
MINNESOTA WILD

1. The Minnesota Wild have done this a few times, what type of water did the Wild ask fans to bring to the Xcel Energy Center for the team to play on?

2. Who scored the Minnesota Wild's first regular season goal?

3. In 2012, what two Minnesota natives were signed to identical contracts?

4. What was Brent Burns's nickname during his time with the Minnesota Wild?

5. Who was the Minnesota Wild's longest-serving captain in team history?

6. What state are both of the Wild's affiliate teams based in?

7. Who became the first Wild player to have a number retired in his honor in 2022?

8. Who was the Wild's first round pick in 2012?

9. Who leads the Wild in all-time goals scored?

10. Who holds the record for most points in their rookie season for the Wild?

ROUND 32

MONTREAL CANADIENS

1. Predating the NHL, what year was the Canadiens founded?

2. What does the "H" in the Montreal Canadiens logo stand for and what is the nickname given to the team by mistake because of the "H" in the logo?

3. Who did the Canadiens beat in 1916 to win their first Stanley Cup?

4. What Canadiens goalie holds the franchise single-season record for wins?

5. Who became the Montreal Canadiens captain after Max Pacioretty was traded to the Vegas Golden Knights?

6. Which prominent Canadian family owns the team?

7. When is the last time the Canadiens won a Stanley Cup?

8. True or False: The Canadiens are the first NHL to have 3,000 all-time wins?

9. Between 1979 to 1995, who did the Canadiens play in the "Battle of Quebec"?

10. Who was the team captain from 2010-2014?

ROUND 33 — NASHVILLE PREDATORS

1. In what round did the Nashville Predators take Pekka Rinne?

2. What country singer is former Nashville Predators captain Mike Fisher married to?

3. What Predators goalie is one of two goalies in NHL history to be credited with a goal in both the AHL and NHL?

4. Who was the coach of the Predators when the team won their 2017-2018 Presidents Trophy?

5. What type of fish do Predators fans throw onto the ice that some have deemed as an "instrument of crime"?

6. What do the Predators fans smash outside of their arena from time to time?

7. Who is the most recent Predators goalie to score a goal?

8. Who leads the Predators in all-time games played?

9. Who holds the record for most goals in their rookie season with the Predators?

10. What country is the Predators captain Roman Josi from?

ROUND 34 — NEW JERSEY DEVILS

1. What was Scott Stevens's nickname?

2. What was the name of the New Jersey Devils coach who told referee Don Koharski to "have another donut"?

3. Who did the New Jersey Devils beat to win their first Stanley Cup in 1995?

4. Who was the first Devil to win Rookie of the Year?

5. What state was Devils' first round pick Scott Gomez born in?

6. What is the New Jersey Devils named after?

7. How many Stanley Cups have the Devils won?

8. Who was the Devils' captain from 2007-2011?

9. What was the name of the team when they were located in Kansas from 1974-76?

10. What is the nickname of the Prudential Center?

ROUND 35

NEW YORK ISLANDERS

1. What year did the New York Islanders join the NHL?

2. Who did the Islanders beat to win their first Stanley Cup in 1980?

3. What round did the Islanders draft Anders Lee in 2009?

4. Who was the first Islanders goalie to post a shutout in his first game with the team?

5. Who was the Islanders' general manager who traded Zdeno Chara?

6. Why have the Islanders been called a "nomadic team"?

7. What was the name of the two Arenas the Islanders called home in 2019?

8. Who was the Islanders' first captain?

9. How many Stanley Cups have the Islanders won?

10. True or False: The Islanders have won a President's Trophy.

ROUND 36: NEW YORK RANGERS

1. In what decade did the Rangers win their first Stanley Cup?

2. What has been handed out to a player in the locker room after each New York Rangers victory since 2011?

3. Who was the Rangers captain after Ryan Callahan left the team in 2014?

4. What was Henrik Lundqvist's nickname?

5. What is the name of the Rangers coach with the most wins in franchise history?

6. True or False: A common joke amongst NHL fans is that the Rangers play in a train station.

7. What is the nickname for Madison Square Garden?

8. Who was the Rangers Captain from 2008-2011?

9. Who did the Rangers pick 20th overall in the 2008 NHL Draft?

10. True or False: Eric Lindros played for the New York Rangers?

ROUND 37 — OTTAWA SENATORS

1. Who was the first Ottawa Senators player to be selected in the NHL Draft?

2. Who became team captain of the Senators after Daniel Alfredsson went to Detroit in free agency?

3. Who did the Senators get in return when they traded Alexei Yashin to the New York Islanders?

4. Who was the first Senators player to win Rookie of the Year?

5. How many years was there between the end of the original Ottawa Senators team and the start of the current franchise? 6, 26, 36 or 56?

6. What did the Senators give up for Matt Duchene in the 2017 three-team trade?

7. How many Stanley Cups have the Senators won as a new franchise?

8. Whose #4 sweater was retired by the Senators in 2020?

9. Who is the only Senator to win two Selkie Trophies?

10. Who is the Senator's cross-province rival?

ROUND 38
PHILADELPHIA FLYERS

1. Who was the first Philadelphia Flyers captain in team history?

2. What players made up the "Legion of Doom"?

3. Who was the Flyers' captain before Claude Giroux?

4. What international team did the Flyers chase off the ice in 1976?

5. What team were the Philadelphia Flyers playing when both teams broke the record for most penalty minutes in one game during the 2003-2004 season?

6. Who was the goalie for the Flyers during their 2 Stanley Cups?

7. Which former center had his number 88 retired in 2018, 18 years after his last appearance for the team?

8. What former Flyer won the Calder Cup with the Phantoms and later captained the team?

9. What QMJHL team did Claude Giroux play juniors for?

10. What current Flyer has a record 7 Toyota Cup Trophies?

ROUND 39
PITTSBURGH PENGUINS

1. Who did the Penguins defeat to win their first Stanley Cup in 1991?

2. What was the first number retired by the Pittsburgh Penguins?

3. Who is the youngest team captain to win the Stanley Cup and how old was he?

4. What was the first NHL team to play in Pittsburgh?

5. What was the nickname of the Pittsburgh Penguins Civic Arena before it was demolished in 2012?

6. What team has been the Penguins ECHL affiliate since 2000-2001?

7. What are the two numbers retired by the Penguins?

8. What number is unofficially retired by the Penguins and will not be worn by another player?

9. What was the first name of PPG Paints Arena?

10. Who did the Penguins beat to win the 2017 Stanley Cup?

ROUND 40
SAN JOSE SHARKS

1. Who was the first San Jose Sharks player to score over 50 goals in one season?

2. Who was the first player to win the Hart Memorial Trophy during a season where he played for two different teams?

3. Why was the line of Joe Pavelski, Kyle Wellwood, and Torrey Mitchell called "The Helicopter Line"?

4. What former Sharks goalie holds the record for most wins in one season?

5. Who was the Sharks' first captain in franchise history?

6. Who was the Sharks' captain from 1998 to 2003?

7. What year did the Sharks win their only President's Trophy?

8. Who did the Sharks lose to in their only Stanley Cup appearance in 2016?

9. What current Shark was in two episodes of Vikings?

10. Where did Logan Couture play his Juniors?

ROUND 41

SEATTLE KRAKEN

1. Who scored the first goal in Seattle Kraken history?

2. Who scored the first goal in the Climate Pledge Arena?

3. What type of animal is native to Puget Sound, partially responsible for the team's name?

4. Besides Wayne Gretzky's number, what is the only number retired by the Seattle Kraken and why?

5. What is the names of both brothers that were drafted by the Seattle Kraken in the expansion draft?

6. Who owns the naming rights to the Climate Pledge Arena?

7. Who was the first team captain in Kraken's history?

8. What was the name of Climate Pledge Arena before the renovation?

9. What team did the Kraken beat for their first NHL win?

10. What year was the team founded?

ROUND 42 — ST. LOUIS BLUES

1. On January 3rd, 2019, what place was the St. Louis Blues in the table before rebounding their season and eventually winning the Stanley Cup?

2. Who holds the record for franchise most goals in a single season?

3. What St. Louis Blues player scored a goal in four consecutive Stanley Cup Finals games?

4. What is the name of the former St. Louis Blues goalie who holds the record for most single-season shutout victories?

5. Who was the player the St. Louis Blues selected in their only franchise first overall pick in the 2006 NHL Entry Draft?

6. How many Stanley Cup appearances do the Blues have?

7. What former Blues player was the third American player to score 500 goals?

8. Who was Blues' captain from 2020-2023 before he joined the Maple Leafs?

9. Who did the Blues defeat to win their first Stanley Cup?

10. Who did the Blues select 8th overall in the 2008 NHL draft?

ROUND 43

TAMPA BAY LIGHTNING

1. Who scored the winning goal for the lightening in the 2021 Stanley Cup?

2. Who is the tallest goalie in NHL history who played the bulk of his career in Tampa?

3. Whose number was the first number retired by the Tampa Bay Lightning and what was it?

4. Who was the first Lightning player to score 60 goals in a single season?

5. Where did Vincent Lecavalier sign in free agency after the Lightning bought him out?

6. What is the name of the Lightning mascot?

7. What is the name of the player that faced the Lightning in two Stanley Cups and then signed with them in 2021?

8. Who was the Tampa Bay Lightning's first Captain?

9. What two players were inducted to the Tampa Bay Lightning Hall of Fame in 2017?

10. Who is the Tampa Bay Lightning's all-time leading scorer for defensemen?

ROUND 44: TORONTO MAPLE LEAFS

1. What is the name of the Maple Leaf whose nickname was "Superman"?

2. True or false: The Maple Leafs are the only NHL team to lose to a Zamboni driver?

3. What is the name of the Maple Leafs' captain that cut the "C" from his jersey?

4. Who was the first European captain in not only Maple Leafs but NHL history?

5. In 1985, who was the Maple Leafs' only first overall draft pick until Auston Matthews in 2017?

6. Name one of the two names the Leafs went by before 1927?

7. How many Conference championships have the Maple Leafs won?

8. Who is the only current Leaf player to be in the top ten for points per game?

9. Who was the team captain before John Tavares?

10. Who leads the Maple Leafs in all-time games played?

ROUND 45
VANCOUVER CANUCKS

1. Who scored the first goal in Vancouver Canucks history back in 1970?

2. How many Stanley Cups have the Nucks reached?

3. Who was the Nuks goalie after Mark Messier left the team?

4. Who holds the single season record for penalty minutes for the Nucks?

5. Who was the first Nuck to get 80 assists in one season?

6. What were the names of the twins drafted by the Nucks 2nd and 3rd overall in the 1999 NHL Draft?

7. What Philadelphia Flyer is former Nucks captain Bo Horvat's cousin?

8. Who has a statue commemorated to them outside of Rodgers Arena for literally waving the white flag?

9. Who was the first Nuck to win the Calder Memorial Trophy?

10. Who did the Nucks draft 10th overall in the 2019 Draft?

ROUND 46: VEGAS GOLDEN KNIGHTS

1. What is the only number retired by the Vegas Golden Knights?

2. Who was the first Vegas Golden Knights player to reach 50 assists in one season?

3. What is the nickname for the T-Mobile arena?

4. Why did Bill Foley name the team the Vegas Golden Knights?

5. Who is the first captain in Vegas Golden Knight's history?

6. What two Knights goalies won the William M. Jennings Trophy in 2021?

7. Who scored the most goals in a single season for the Golden Knights in 2017-2018?

8. Who is the youngest player to score a goal in Vegas Golden Knights history?

9. Who was the first player taken by the Golden Knights in the expansion draft?

10. Who did the Golden Knights trade Cody Glass for?

ROUND 47
WASHINGTON CAPITALS

1. What Capitals player has won the Maurice "Rocket" Richard Trophy a record nine times?

2. What former Capitals player was nicknamed "Secretary of Defense"?

3. What Russian club did NHL great Alexander Ovechkin play for before entering the NHL and again in 2012-13?

4. What Capitals player was given the penalty box from MCI Center when they team moved arenas and retired his number?

5. Who was the first player in hockey history to win the Kelly Cup (ECHL), Calder Cup (AHL) and Stanley Cup?

6. Who did the Capitals beat to win their first Stanley Cup?

7. Who is the only player in Capitals history to win the Calder Memorial Trophy?

8. When was Evgeny Kuznetsov's first NHL season?

9. Who did the Capitals draft 29th overall in the 2004 NHL Draft?

10. How many Presidents Trophies have the Capitals won?

ROUND 48
WINNIPEG JETS

1. Who scored the first goal for the Winnipeg Jets when they returned to Winnipeg in 2011?

2. Who did the Jets draft in their first draft in Winnipeg 7th overall in 2011?

3. How many Jets players are still around from the Atlanta days and who are they?

4. Who was the first Jets goalie to record three shutouts in a row?

5. What color are Jets fans asked to wear to home playoff games?

6. Who are the Jets' AHL affiliate who play in the same arena?

7. Who are the only two captains in the Jets' "2.0" history?

8. Who is the leader in goals for the Winnipeg Jets/ Atlanta Thrashers franchise history?

9. Who did the Atlanta Thrashers take in the 2006 NHL draft 12th overall?

10. Where did Kyle Connor play college hockey?

ROUND 49
STANLEY CUP MATCH UPS

Can you name the finalists and winners of the 20 most recent Stanley Cups?

Year	Matchup	Score	Winner
2002	Carolina Hurricanes	1-4	Detroit Red Wings
2003	Mighty Ducks of Anaheim	3-4	New Jersey Devils
2004	Calgary Flames	3-4	Tampa Bay Lightning
2006	Edmonton Oilers	3-4	Carolina Hurricanes
2007	Ottawa Senators	1-4	Anaheim Ducks
2008	Pittsburgh Penguins	2-4	Detroit Red Wings
2009	Detroit Red Wings	3-4	Pittsburgh Penguins
2010	Philadelphia Flyers	2-4	Chicago Blackhawks
2011	Vancouver Canucks	3-4	Boston Bruins
2012	New Jersey Devils	2-4	Los Angeles Kings
2013	Boston Bruins	2-4	Chicago Blackhawks
2014	New York Rangers	1-4	Los Angeles Kings
2015	Tampa Bay Lightning	2-4	Chicago Blackhawks
2016	San Jose Sharks	2-4	Pittsburgh Penguins
2017	Nashville Predators	2-4	Pittsburgh Penguins
2018	Vegas Golden Knights	1-4	Washington Capitals
2019	Boston Bruins	3-4	St. Louis Blues
2020	Dallas Stars	2-4	Tampa Bay Lightning
2021	Montreal Canadiens	1-4	Tampa Bay Lightning
2022	Tampa Bay Lightning	2-4	Colorado Avalanche

ROUND 50
OPENING DAY & NHL DEBUTS

1. The 2016-2017 was the 50th season in Philadelphia Flyers history, who did they play in their home opener?

2. Auston Matthews's debut was opening night in 2016, what team did he score 4 goals against that night?

3. What two seasons did the NHL open in the month of January?

4. There has only been one time in NHL history since 1970 where two new expansion teams played head-to-head on opening night, who were they?

5. Who holds the NHL record for most goals scored in a season-opening game?

6. The first NHL game to be decided by a shootout happened in 2005, what were the teams and who won?

7. The now Buffalo Sabre, Will Butcher made his NHL debut with the New Jersey Devils against the team that drafted him in the 5th round of the 2013 Draft. He put up three points, what was that team?

8. This goalie impressed everyone in 2014 when he made a shutout in his NHL debut for the San Jose Sharks, making him the 22nd goalie in NHL history to do so. Who was that goalie?

9. This former St. Cloud State University scored a hat trick and the shootout winner in his debut game with the Canadiens in 2019, what was his name?

10 Who was the fourth player in NHL history to score a hat trick on their NHL debut in 2010 with the Rangers?

11 This Zamboni driver was the driver for the Maple Leafs arena and even practiced with the Toronto Marlies, he had to sub in for a game against the Maples as the emergency goaltender, what is his name?

12 In 2018 both Chicago Blackhawks goalies Anton Forsberg and Collin Delia both went down with injuries and the Blackhawks had to use the arena's emergency goaltender, stopping all seven shots he faced. Who was he and what is his profession?

13 What Maple Leafs player made his NHL debut in 2016 during the 'Battle of Ontario' and scored 4 goals in that game?

14 Jorge Alves was the emergency goalie for the Carolina Hurricanes in 2016, he was in the game for 7.6 seconds. Does this make him an NHL alumnus?

15 This Nucks player holds the record for the shortest NHL debut in a game against the flames in 2014. Right at the puck drop, he got into a fight and received a five-minute major and a game misconduct, who was this player?

16 Who was the first goalie in NHL history to make his debut and secure a shutout in 65 minutes of play and win the shootout for the Minnesota Wild back in 2006?

ROUND 51 — DRAFTS OF FAMOUS PLAYERS

1. What team drafted Zdeno Chara?

2. What team drafted Vincent Lecavalier?

3. What team drafted Brayden Schenn?

4. What team drafted Tim Thomas?

5. What team drafted St. Louis Blues legend, Brett Hull?

6. What team drafted current New Jersey Devil Dougie Hamilton?

7. Who drafted Tyler Seguin?

8. What now relocated team drafted all-star Dany Heatley?

9. What team drafted "spine like a slinky" Dominik Hasek?

10. What team drafted the "100-million-dollar man" Ilya Kovalchuk?

11. What team drafted Jason Spezza?

12. What now relocated team drafted Jean-Sebastien Giguere?

13. What team drafted "Jumbo" Joe Thornton first overall in 1997?

14) What team drafted three-time Stanley Cup champion Marian Hossa?

15) What team drafted Martin St. Louis?

16) What team drafted legendary Calgary netminder Miikka Kiprusoff?

17) What team drafted arguably the greatest American Hockey player Mike Modano?

18) What team drafted Roberto Luongo 4th overall in 1997?

19) What team drafted Ducks Stanley Cup Champion Scott Niedermayer?

20) What team drafted two-time Stanley Cup winner Phil Kessel?

ROUND 52: OLYMPIC & WORLD CUP TEAMS

1. Who was the captain of the 2022 Canadian Olympic hockey team?

2. Who was the captain of the 2022 United States Olympic hockey team?

3. Who was in nets for Canada during the Gold Medal game against the United States in 2010?

4. Who was in nets for the United States during the Gold Medal game against Canada in 2010?

5. What two United States athletes tied for 3rd in scoring with Jonathan Toews at 8 points during the 2010 Winter Olympics?

6. What year was the first women's edition of Olympic Ice Hockey? 1996, 1998, 2000 or 2002?

7. Who scored the game-winning goal for Canada in the 2010 Winter Olympics Gold Medal game?

8. Which team took home their first-ever Ice Hockey Olympic gold medal in 2022?

9. Name one of the three women who hold the record for the most gold medals of any Canadian Olympian (all ice hockey players).

10. In what place did USA and Canada place in the 2018 Winter Olympics?

11. What country hosted the 2016 World Cup of Hockey and where did they host it?

12. What decade was the first non-Olympic edition of the Ice Hockey World Championships played?

13. When Czechoslovakia split in 1993, which team took over as successor whilst the other was forced to start in the lowest division? Czech Republic or Slovakia?

14. As of 2023, Canada, China and Russia have all won the Word Championships the joint-highest times. How many?

15. How many divisions are there in the World Championships?

16. Name one of the two Finnish cities that hosted the 2022 edition.

17. What country will host the 2024 edition?

18. Considered to be one of the greatest goaltenders in the history of the sport, which Soviet player holds the record for most Championships won with 10?

19. When did the United States and Canada last meet in a World Championship Final? 1960, 1980, 2000 or 2020?

20. Which former nation won nine consecutive World Championships between 1963 and 1971?

ROUND 53: MINOR LEAGUE

1. The Philadelphia Phantoms played in Philadelphia from 1996 to 2009 before their arena was demolished. What were they called before moving to Leigh Valley?

2. What is the oldest team in the American Hockey League?

3. The Hartford Wolfpack have been around since 1926 and have used their current name from 1997-2010 and then from 2013 to present. What did the team briefly change its name to between 2010 and 2013?

4. Who won the first Calder Cup in 1938?

5. What AHL team has won the most Calder Cups at a record 11 times?

6. Who are the only two teams that survived the collapse of the International Hockey League and still play in the same city in the AHL?

7. Who became the AHL's 32nd team when they joined the league in 2022?

8. What team left the ECHL in 2018 to join the AHL, becoming the league's 31st team?

9. In 2020, the San Antonio Rampage were purchased and relocated to Henderson Nevada, what is their new team's name?

10. Over their almost 100-year history, the Hershey Bears have had over 8 NHL affiliates, name two.

11) What is the oldest ECHL Team? (Older than the ECHL itself).

12) What is the name of the award given to the league's MVP since 1948?

13) What two leagues combined to create the East Coast Hockey League?

14) What double AA league did the ECHL fold after they ceased operations in 2003?

15) How many Ray Miron Presidents Cups and Kelly Cups did the Colorado Eagles win before joining the AHL?

16) Who leads AHL history with the most points at 1375?

17) What goalie leads the AHL in most wins at 359?

18) This two-time Los Angeles Kings Stanley Cup champion made his professional debut with the Reading Royals of the ECHL, who was it?

19) Long before winning a Stanley Cup between the pipes with the Washington Capitals, this goalie made his professional debut with the South Carolina Stingrays of the ECHL, who is he?

20) Before the Vegas Golden Knights came to town, for 11 years Vegas was home to another professional hockey team that saw many future NHL players come through, what was the name of that team?

ROUND 54
HALL OF FAME

1. When was the Hockey Hall of Fame (HHoF) established?

2. How many years must you be retired before consideration in the HHoF?

3. True or False: The rule above concerning the HHoF has been broken multiple times.

4. True or False: Mario Lemieux was the first active player to be inducted into the Hockey Hall of Fame?

5. What Hockey Hall of Fame inductee was first to win the Hart Trophy for NHL's Most Valuable Player for three consecutive seasons?

6. Who was the first Hockey Hall of Fame inductee to be named an all-star as both forward and defensemen?

7. How many 50-goal seasons did HHoF inductee Mike Bossy have?

8. Who was the first Russian player to be inducted into the HHoF?

9. Where is the Hockey Hall of Fame located?

10. Does the NHL and IIHF own the Hockey Hall of Fame?

11. What was the building that Hockey Hall of Fame resides in originally?

12. True or False: The original Stanley Cup is located in the former banks vault.

13. To the nearest 100, how many players are currently in the Hockey Hall of Fame?

14. Are there players in the Hockey Hall of Fame who did not play in the NHL?

15. What Canadian Province has the most players inducted into the Hockey Hall of Fame?

16. What is the Hockey Hall of Fame called in French?

17. Which Slovakian was the only non-Canadian inducted in 2020?

18. True or False: The Hockey Hall of Fame has a dedicated category for players whose careers were tragically cut short and are inducted posthumously.

19. True or False: There are no females honored in the Hockey Hall of Fame in almost 100 years of existence.

20. Where has the Hockey Hall of Fame held all its induction ceremonies since 1993?

ROUND 55
NHL DRAFTS FIRSTS

1. Who was the first NHL player drafted from Australia?

2. Who was the first player to be drafted from Estonia?

3. Who was the first player to be drafted from Nigeria?

4. Who was the first player to be drafted from the United States?

5. Who was the first player drafted from Czechoslovakia (now defunct)?

6. Who was the first player drafted from the Soviet Union?

7. Who was the first player drafted from Slovenia?

8. Who was the first player drafted from Japan?

9. Who was the first player drafted from Brunei?

10. Who was the first player drafted from Bulgaria?

ROUND 56 — NCAA HOCKEY

1. What NCAA team has the most NHL drafted players in the first round?

2. How many first overall draft picks have come from the NCAA since 1963? 2, 12, 22 or 32?

3. What is the Frozen Four?

4. What NCAA hockey conference has the most drafted players?

5. Who is the number one ranked goalie in Penn State Hockey history? (Hint: his first NHL contract was with the Avalanche).

6. Who was the most recent first overall pick to be drafted by an NHL team from the NCAA?

7. Where did Zach Parise play college hockey?

8. What is the Hobey Baker Award?

9. Cale Makar won the Hobey Baker in 2019, what NHL trophy did he win the next year in 2020?

10. Who is the only Hobey Baker Award winner to be inducted into the Hockey Hall of Fame?

ROUND 57 — ARENAS I

How well do you know your NHL arenas?
Write the correct team on each row.

Arena	Capacity	Team
KeyBank Center	19,070	
Bridgestone Arena	17,159	
Crypto.com Arena	18,230	
Canadian Tire Centre	19,347	
Rogers Place	18,347	
Mullett Arena	4,600	
PPG Paints Arena	18,387	
Amalie Arena	19,092	
Little Caesars Arena	19,515	
Enterprise Center	18,096	
Xcel Energy Center	17,954	
United Center	19,717	
Madison Square Garden	18,006	
Scotiabank Saddledome	19,289	
FLA Live Arena	19,250	
UBS Arena	17,255	

ROUND 58
ARENAS II

Here are the next 16, good luck!

Arena	Capacity	Team
Honda Center	17,174	
Prudential Center	16,514	
Rogers Arena	18,910	
SAP Center	17,562	
Capital One Arena	18,573	
PNC Arena	18,680	
Ball Arena	17,809	
Nationwide Arena	18,144	
T-Mobile Arena	17,367	
American Airlines Center	18,532	
Canada Life Centre	15,321	
Scotiabank Arena	18,800	
Bell Centre	21,105	
TD Garden	17,565	
Wells Fargo Center	19,538	
Climate Pledge Arena	17,151	

ANSWERS

10. Sidney Crosby
11. Gordie Howe
12. The Detroit Red Wings
13. Minnesota
14. Beer
15. French fries, cheese curds, gravy, and butter
16. Miracle
17. Twelve
18. Freeze them
19. Vulcanized rubber
20. 1959

Warm-Up II

Atlantic	Central
Florida Panthers	Colorado Avalanche
Toronto Maple Leafs	Minnesota Wild
Tampa Bay Lightning	St. Louis Blues
Boston Bruins	Dallas Stars
Buffalo Sabres	Nashville Predators
Detroit Red Wings	Winnipeg Jets
Ottawa Senators	Chicago Blackhawks
Montreal Canadiens	Arizona Coyotes

Metropolitan	Pacific
Carolina Hurricanes	Calgary Flames
New York Rangers	Edmonton Oilers
Pittsburgh Penguins	Los Angeles Kings
Washington Capitals	Vegas Golden Knights
New York Islanders	Vancouver Canucks
Columbus Blue Jackets	San Jose Sharks
New Jersey Devils	Anaheim Ducks
Philadelphia Flyers	Seattle Kraken

Round 1 - Founding & History

1. 1917
2. The National Hockey Association
3. The Boston Bruins
4. Boston Bruins, New York Rangers, Chicago Black Hawks, Detroit Red Wings, Montreal Canadiens, New York Rangers, and Toronto Maple Leafs
5. The Philadelphia Flyers
6. Montreal Maroons
7. Georges Vezina
8. New York Americans
9. Toronto St. Patricks
10. Pacific Coast Hockey Association and Western Canada Hockey League
11. The Pittsburgh Pirates
12. Philadelphia Quakers
13. Maurice Richard
14. Montreal Hockey Club and Ottawa Hockey Club, Montreal won
15. Montreal Canadiens beat the Quebec Bulldogs 16-3
16. 'Phantom' Joe Malone
17. The Great Depression
18. Canadian Expeditionary Force
19. The Windsor Hotel in Montreal
20. Dave Ritchie of the Montreal Wanderers

Round 2 - Stanley Cup
1. Lord Stanley of Preston
2. Dominion Hockey Challenge Cup- later renamed
3. 1893
4. The Seattle Metropolitans
5. The Montreal Canadiens
6. Charlie Gardner of the Chicago Blackhawks in 1934
7. Ken Morrow
8. 9
9. 1919
10. The St. Louis Blues
11. Maurice Richard
12. BOSTON BRUINS
13. Adam Deadmarch
14. Guy Carbonneau
15. 34.5 pounds
16. Peter Forsberg
17. Sylvian Lefebvre
18. 250
19. True
20. Maurice Richard

Round 3 - Trophy Names & History
1. Prince Edward, the Prince of Wales
2. Third president of the NHL
3. 1985-1986 season
4. The Professional Hockey Writers' Association
5. Sportsmanship
6. The NHL general managers of all 32 teams
7. Frank Calder, first NHL president
8. The Pittsburgh Penguins
9. Bobby Orr
10. Patrick Roy
11. He is the only NHL player to die as a result of injuries during a game
12. The members of the NHLPA
13. The head coach
14. Former general manager of the Maple Leafs and Canadiens
15. Patrick Roy and Martin Brodeur
16. Players who best exemplify leadership qualities on and off the ice and contribute to their communities
17. Lead the NHL in goals scored
18. Mark Messier
19. 2019 following the death of Jim Gregory
20. The draft prospect who best exemplifies their commitment to excellence on and off the ice

Round 4 - Coaches
1. Scotty Bowman
2. Nine
3. Patrick Roy
4. Marc Crawford
5. Jack Adams
6. Fred Shero
7. Al Arbour
8. The Phoenix Coyotes
9. Pat Burns
10. Jacques Demers
11. Pat Quinn
12. Ned Harkness
13. The New York Rangers
14. $30,000
15. He punched a fan
16. Roger Neilson
17. Jon Cooper
18. Barry Trotz
19. Gerard Gallant
20. Dave Hakstol

Round 5 - General Managers
1. David Poile
2. Kevin Cheveldayoff
3. George McPhee
4. Ron Francis
5. Lou Lamoriello
6. Garth Snow
7. Pierre Lacroix
8. Jack Adams
9. Bryan Murray
10. Glen Sather
11. Sam Pollock

12. Jarmo Kekalainen
13. Kelly McCrimmon
14. John Chayka
15. Don Maloney
16. Scotty Bowman
17. Mike Milbury
18. Don Waddell
19. Craig Button
20. Russ Farwell

Round 6 - Expansion & Relocation
1. Quebec Nordiques, Winnipeg Jets, Hartford Whalers and Edmonton Oilers
2. Winnipeg Jets
3. Hartford Whalers
4. California Seals, Los Angeles Kings, Minnesota North Stars, Philadelphia Flyers, Pittsburgh Penguins and St. Louis Blues?
5. The Colorado Rockies
6. Vancouver Canucks and Buffalo Sabres
7. Denver and Kansas City
8. Cleveland Barons and Columbus Blue Jackets
9. Dallas
10. Nashville Predators
11. Columbus Blue Jackets and Minnesota Wild
12. Cleveland Barons
13. The Vegas Golden Knights
14. The Washington Capitals
15. Reid Duke
16. Dallas Stars- North Stars and Barons merger
17. Tomas Nosek
18. The Hampton Roads Rhinos
19. Kansas City, Missouri
20. Atlanta, Georgia

Round 7 - Player Stats & Records
1. Patrick Marleau
2. Wayne Gretzky
3. Wayne Gretzky
4. Jaromir Jagr
5. Tiger Williams

6. Larry Robinson
7. Tie Domi
8. Raffi Torres
9. Chris Chelios and Gordie Howe
10. Mark Messier
11. 52-years-old
12. 11 Stanley Cups
13. Auston Matthews - 6 goals
14. Mario Lemieux
15. William Karlsson - 43 goals
16. Ray Bourque
17. Pekka Rinne
18. Ron Hextall
19. Mike Sillinger
20. Dave Schultz

Round 8 - Wayne Gretzky
1. The Indianapolis Racers
2. In a plane while the GM worked on a deal.
3. No, they were eliminated by the Winnipeg Jets in six games.
4. Peterborough Petes and Sault Ste. Marie Greyhounds.
5. 215 points
6. Edmonton Oilers, Los Angeles Kings, St. Louis Blues and New York Rangers.
7. No, he did not, in 1998 Canada finished 4th.
8. 3
9. 4
10. Jim Carson, Martin Gelinas, three-first round picks and $15 million in cash.
11. His teammate in juniors already had #9 and his coach suggested #99.
12. 3 times
13. 8 straight trophies.
14. 39 games
15. 61 records
16. The Toronto Sun
17. 110 points
18. 1999
19. 4
20. Dave Semanko or Marty McSorley.

Round 9 - Mario Lemieux

1. Laval Voisins
2. 1984
3. 1,022
4. 10
5. 3
6. 5
7. The Philadelphia Flyers
8. True
9. 1999 and to save them from bankruptcy, the team also owed him millions in deferred salary.
10. Sidney Crosby
11. True
12. 4
13. 12 games
14. 49
15. To show respect to Gretzky.
16. True
17. False, the highest was 199 points.
18. Even-strength, short-handed, power play, penalty shot and empty net goals.
19. 2002 Winter Olympics at Salt Lake City, Utah.
20. The Magnificent One, Le Magnifique or Super Mario.

Round 10 - First Overall Draft Picks I

Year	Team	Player
2003	Pittsburgh Penguins	Marc-Andre Fleury
2004	Washington Capitals	Alexander Ovechkin
2005	Pittsburgh Penguins	Sidney Crosby
2006	St. Louis Blues	Erik Johnson
2007	Chicago Blackhawks	Patrick Kane
2008	Tampa Bay Lightning	Steven Stamkos
2009	New York Islanders	John Tavares
2010	Edmonton Oilers	Taylor Hall
2011	Edmonton Oilers	Ryan Nugent-Hopkins
2012	Edmonton Oilers	Nail Yakupov
2013	Colorado Avalanche	Nathan MacKinnon
2014	Florida Panthers	Aaron Ekblad
2015	Edmonton Oilers	Connor McDavid
2016	Toronto Maple Leafs	Auston Matthews
2017	New Jersey Devils	Nico Hischier
2018	Buffalo Sabres	Rasmus Dahlin
2019	New Jersey Devils	Jack Hughes
2020	New York Rangers	Alexis Lafreniere
2021	Buffalo Sabres	Owen Power
2022	Montreal Canadiens	Juraj Slafkovsky

Round 11 - Hockey TV & Movie Trivia
1. Kurt Russell
2. Doug Smith
3. Mike Modano
4. Tyler Seguin
5. The New York Rangers
6. Paul Newman
7. 16, 17, and 18
8. David Hanson played 11 games for the Detroit Red Wings in 1978-79
9. Marc-Andre Fleury
10. Georges Laraque
11. Peter Zesel
12. Keanu Reeves
13. Mike Rupp
14. Wyatt Russell played hockey for multiple years before following his fathers' footsteps
15. Letterkenny Irish or Letterkenny Shamrocks
16. The Kent County Eagles
17. The Philadelphia Flyers
18. Hendrix Sports
19. Gordon Bombay
20. Trailer Park Boys

10. Sergei Makarov played his first season at 31 years old and won rookie of the year.
11. A player will get a game misconduct if a jersey comes off during a fight for not having the fighting strap on, unless ripped by the other player.
12. Matt Cooke hit Marc Savard clearly in the head, illegal checks to the head as principle point of conduct results in a 5-minute penalty and a game misconduct.
13. If a player comes overseas midseason he must pass through waivers before a team can sign him. It is because Reijo Ruotsalaninen came over mid-season and helped the Oilers win a Cup.
14. Phil Esposito
15. Martin Broduer
16. Ted Lindsay
17. The Montreal Canadiens
18. Jacques Plante
19. Sidney Crosby
20. Matt Duchene

Round 12 - Rule Changes
1. Pulling the goalie for an extra man.
2. Waving the stick in Martin Broduer's face, now players must face away from the goalie while screening.
3. Other NHL teams complained that Durnan leaving his to talk to officials slowed the game to much.
4. Roberto Luongo
5. Bill Barber
6. Gary Smith
7. The Oilers would purposely try to get coincidental penalties for Gretzky to have more room out on the ice. This rule makes those calls offsetting.
8. Bobby Hull and Stan Mikita would use funky curves on their sticks so the puck shots would confuse goalies.
9. Brett Hull scored the 1999 Stanley Cup winning goal with his skate in the crease, due to insane backlash the NHL removed the rule.

Round 13 - NHL Points Leaders

Rank	Team(s)	GP	Points	Player
1	EDM, LAK, STL, NYR	1,514	2,857	Wayne Gretzky
2	PIT, WSH, NYR, PHI, DAL, BOS, NJD, FLA, CGY	1,733	1,921	Jaromir Jagr
3	EDM, NYR, VAN	1,756	1,887	Mark Messier
4	DET, HFD	1,767	1,850	Gordie Howe
5	HFD, PIT, CAR, TOR	1,731	1,798	Ron Francis
6	DET, LAK, NYR	1,348	1,771	Marcel Dionne
7	DET	1,514	1,755	Steve Yzerman
8	PIT	915	1,723	Mario Lemieux
9	QUE, COL	1,378	1,641	Joe Sakic
10	CHI, BOS, NYR	1,282	1,590	Phil Esposito
11	BOS, COL	1,612	1,579	Ray Bourque
12	BOS, SJS, TOR, FLA	1,714	1,539	Joe Thornton
13	PIT, PHI, MTL, CAR, ATL, TBL, BOS	1,652	1,533	Mark Recchi
14	EDM, PIT, LAK, DET, HFD, PHI, CHI, CAR, BOS	1,409	1,531	Paul Coffey
15	PIT	1,185	1,497	Sidney Crosby
16	WSH	1,345	1,483	Alex Ovechkin
17	CHI	1,396	1,467	Stan Mikita
18	WIN, ANA, SJS, COL	1,451	1,457	Teemu Selanne
19	NYI, PIT	1,279	1,425	Bryan Trottier
20	DET, STL, BOS, WSH, PHI, ANA, EDM	1,337	1,420	Adam Oates

Round 14 - Mascots

1. The Detroit Red Wings- Al the Octopus.
2. New York Rangers, Seattle Kraken, Detroit Red Wings.
3. New York Rangers
4. Gritty
5. St. Bernard dog
6. It's the average temperature in Los Angeles.
7. Back in the day it only took 8 wins to win the Cup, hence the eight tentacles.
8. Bear
9. The Maple Leafs Garden was at 60 Carlton Street.
10. Gila monster.
11. Slapshot, he was around for one season in 1976.
12. Siberian Husky or Alaskan Malamute.
13. It is the year the Arizona Coyotes moved from Winnipeg.
14. Orca or killer whale.
15. The Edmonton Oilers and he is a Canadian Lynx.
16. The Pittsburgh Penguins mascot is almost a twin to the Wilkes Barre Scranton Penguins mascot.
17. Mick E. Moose and Benny.
18. 18,001 because of the 18,000 fans who attend Wild games.
19. Stanley C. Panther and Viktor E. Rat.
20. Youppi! He was originally the mascot for the Montreal Expos.

Year	Team	Player
1983	Minnesota North Stars	Brian Lawton
1984	Pittsburgh Penguins	Mario Lemieux
1985	Toronto Maple Leafs	Wendel Clark
1986	Detroit Red Wings	Joe Murphy
1987	Buffalo Sabres	Pierre Turgeon
1988	Minnesota North Stars	Mike Modano
1989	Quebec Nordiques	Mats Sundin
1990	Quebec Nordiques	Owen Nolan
1991	Quebec Nordiques	Eric Lindros
1992	Tampa Bay Lightning	Roman Hamrlik
1993	Ottawa Senators	Alexandre Daigle
1994	Florida Panthers	Ed Jovanovski
1995	Ottawa Senators	Bryan Berard
1996	Ottawa Senators	Chris Phillips
1997	Boston Bruins	Joe Thornton
1998	Tampa Bay Lightning	Vincent Lecavalier
1999	Atlanta Thrashers	Patrik Stefan
2000	New York Islanders	Rick DiPietro
2001	Atlanta Thrashers	Ilya Kovalchuk
2002	Columbus Blue Jackets	Rick Nash

Round 16 - NHL Draft Steals
1. Kirill Kaprizov
2. Brayden Point
3. Alex DeBrincat
4. Mathew Barzal
5. Brendan Gallagher
6. Victor Arvidsson
7. Johnny "Hockey" Gaudreau
8. Dominik Hasek
9. Pavel Datsyuk
10. Henrik Lundqvist
11. Henrik Zetterberg
12. Mark Messier
13. Nicklas Lidstrom
14. Mikka Kiprusoff
15. Mathew Barzal
16. Jari Kurri
17. Brad Richards
18. Current captain Jamie Benn
19. Joe Pavelski
20. Jaroslav Halak and Brian Elliott

Round 17 - Anaheim Ducks
1. Troy Loney
2. No, he did not, he joined the team next season.
3. He wore #35.
4. The Ottawa Senators
5. Ryan Getzlaf
6. 1993
7. The Norfolk Admirals
8. Teemu Selanne, Paul Kariya and Scott Niedermayer.
9. Paul Kariya
10. Ryan Getzlaf

Round 18 - Arizona Coyotes
1. Ilya Bryzgalov
2. Teemu Selanne
3. Shane Doan #19.
4. Keith Tkachuk, Teppo Numminen, Shane Done and Oliver Ekman Larsson.
5. Dale Hawerchuk
6. The Tucson Roadrunners.
7. 2011-2012 Division championship.
8. Shane Doan
9. Philadelphia Flyers
10. Max Domi

Round 19 - Boston Bruins
1. They were the first American franchise founded in 1924.
2. 1970 and the St. Louis Blues.
3. In respect to Phil Esposito.
4. Willie O'Ree
5. Joe Thornton, Glen Murray, and Mike Knuble.
6. 11
7. Phil Esposito
8. Ray Bourque
9. Providence Bruins
10. 2008

Round 20 - Buffalo Sabres
1. Gilbert Perreault, Rick Martin, and Rene Robert.
2. Punch Imlach
3. Clint Malarchuk
4. The Cookie Monster
5. Ryan Miller
6. Terry Pegula
7. 0
8. Dominik Hasek
9. 2006-2007
10. Jason Pominville

Round 21 - Calgary Flames
1. Lanny McDonald #9 in 1990.
2. The Montreal Canadiens in 6 games.
3. Jarome Iginla
4. Sergei Makarov
5. The Magic Man
6. The Flames alternative logo.
7. Mark Giordano
8. Jarome Iginla
9. Theoren Fleury
10. 1

Round 22 - Carolina Hurricanes
1. Jeff Skinner in 2010-2011.
2. The Edmonton Oilers- first major professional title in North Carolina History.
3. "Bunch of Jerks"
4. David Ayers and the Toronto Maple Leafs.
5. Niclas Wallin
6. 2005-2006
7. Rod Brind'Amor
8. 3, Blues, Flyers and Hurricanes.
9. Eric Staal
10. Ron Francis

Round 23 - Chicago Blackhawks
1. Joe Sakic
2. 1933-1934
3. Stan Mikita and 22 years.
4. Chris Chelios - 1,495 penalty minutes.
5. The Golden Jet
6. Kris Versteeg
7. Black Hawk, a Native American Chief who served in the Army.
8. Chelsea Dagger
9. Stan Mikita
10. The Philadelphia Flyers

Round 24 - Colorado Avalanche
1. Claude Lemieux
2. 9 consecutive division titles from 1974-1982.
3. Peter Stastny, Peter Forsberg, Chris Drury, Gabriel Landeskog, Nathan MacKinnon, and Cale Makar.
4. Milan Hejduk
5. The New Jersey Devils and the Florida Panthers.
6. The Pepsi Center
7. 88
8. Joe Sakic, Adam Foote, Milan Hejduk and Gabriel Landeskog.
9. "The Three Headed Monster"
10. Milan Hejduk

Round 25 - Columbus Blue Jackets
1. Artemi Panarin
2. 16 consecutive games.
3. The 6th round of the 2008 Draft 157th overall.
4. Goalie Steve Mason.
5. The Montreal Canadiens
6. The Tampa Bay Lightning
7. Sergei Bobrobsky
8. Rick Nash
9. The Civil War.
10. Lyle Odelein

Round 26 - Dallas Stars
1. 1993
2. Mike Modano
3. The Buffalo Sabres
4. Joe Nieuwendyk
5. Marty Turco
6. Sergei Zubov
7. Neal Broten
8. Valeri Nichushkin
9. The Detroit Red Wings
10. Jere Lehtinen

Round 27 - Detroit Red Wings
1. Detroit Cougars and the Detroit Falcons.
2. Steve Yzerman for over 1300 games.
3. Bob Probert and Joey Kocur.
4. 32 times.
5. Colorado Avalanche
6. Sergei Fedorov, Vladimir Kostantinov, Slava Kozlov, Slava Fetisov and Igor Larionov.
7. Nicklas Lidstrom
8. 19
9. Detroit Olympia
10. Mike Ilitch

Round 28 - Edmonton Oilers
1. Kevin Lowe in 1979.
2. Sam Gagner
3. Peter Pocklington
4. The Alberta Oilers
5. Andrew Ference
6. Leon Draisaitl
7. Steve Smith
8. Calgary Flames
9. 8
10. Rexall Place

Round 29 - Florida Panthers
1. 1993
2. Bobby Clarke
3. 20 rounds. Bonus: Nick Bjugstad
4. Rats
5. Jonathan Huberdeau
6. Sunrise, Florida
7. Florida State Flag.
8. Aleksander Barkov
9. Spencer Knight
10. Roberto Luongo

Round 30 - Los Angeles Kings
1. Dave Taylor, Charlie Simmer, Marcel Dionne.
2. The New Jersey Devils and the New York Rangers.
3. Terry Sawchuk
4. Jonathan Quick
5. Anze Kopitar
6. Dustin Brown
7. The San Jose Sharks.
Bonus: Leafs, Islanders, Flyers, Kings.
8. Darryl Sutter
9. Marcel Dionne
10. False

Round 31 - Minnesota Wild
1. Water from local ponds and lakes.
2. Marion Gaborik
3. Zach Parise and Ryan Suter.
4. "Chewbacca"
5. Mikko Koivu
6. Iowa
7. 1
Bonus: To honor their fans who helped bring hockey back to Minnesota.
8. Matt Dumba
9. Marian Gaborik
10. Kirill Kaprizov

Round 32 - Montreal Canadiens
1. 1909
2. Hockey, they got the nickname "Habs".
3. The Portland Rosebuds
4. Carey Price with 44 wins.
5. Shea Weber
6. The Molson Family.
7. 1993
8. True
9. The Nordiques
10. Brian Gionta

Round 33 - Nashville Predators
1. The 8th round
2. Carrie Underwood
3. Chris Mason
4. Peter Laviolette
5. Catfish
6. Cars
7. Pekke Rinne
8. David Legwand
9. Filip Forsberg
Bonus: The Washington Capitals
10. Switzerland

Round 34 - New Jersey Devils
1. "Captain Crunch"
2. Jim Schoenfeld
3. The Detroit Red Wings
4. Martin Brodeur
5. Alaska
6. The mythological creature of the same name.
7. 3
8. Jamie Langenbrunner
9. The Scouts
10. "The Rock"

Round 35 - New York Islanders
1. 1972
2. The Philadelphia Flyers
3. The 6th round in 2009
4. Robin Lehner
5. Mike Milbury
6. They have had multiple home arenas on Long Island.
7. Nassau Coliseum and Barclays Center.
8. Ed Westfall
9. 4 consecutive Cups.
10. False

Round 36 - New York Rangers
1. 1920s (1928)
2. The Broadway Hat
3. Ryan McDonagh
4. King Henrik
5. Emile Francis
6. True
7. "The Garden"
8. Chris Drury
9. Michael Del Zotto
10. True

Round 37 - Ottawa Senators
1. Alexei Yashin
2. Jason Spezza
3. Zdeno Chara, a pick that turned into Jason Spezza and Bill Muckalt.
4. Daniel Alfredsson
5. 56
6. Shane Bowers, Andrew Hammond, a 1st and a 3rd round pick.
7. 0
8. Chris Phillips
9. Erik Karlsson
10. Toronto Maple Leafs

Round 38 - Philadelphia Flyers
1. Lou Angotti
2. Eric Lindors, John LeClair, and Mikael Renberg.
3. Chris Pronger
4. The Red Army.
5. The Ottawa Senators- 419 penalty minutes. Bonus: Keith Yandle
6. Bernie Parent
7. Eric Lindros
8. Mike Richards
9. Gatineau Olympiques
10. Claude Giroux

Round 39 - Pittsburgh Penguins
1. The Minnesota North Stars
2. Mario Lemieux
3. Sidney Crosby and 21.
4. The Pittsburgh Pirates
5. "The Igloo"
6. Wheeling Whalers
7. #21 and #66.
8. #68
9. Consol Energy Center
10. Nashville Predators

Round 40 - San Jose Sharks
1. Jonathan Cheecho
2. Joe Thornton
3. The line was made up of centers and no wings, the name is because helicopters don't have wings.
4. Evgeni Nabokov
5. Doug Wilson - Bonus: Foghorn
6. Owen Nolan
7. 2008-2009
8. The Pittsburgh Penguins
9. Brent Burns
10. The Ottawa 67ers

Round 41 - Seattle Kraken
1. Ryan Donato
2. Vince Dunn
3. Octopus
4. The #32, in honor of the 32nd team and the 32,000 fans who placed deposits on the team.
5. Hayden and Cale Fleury.
6. Amazon
7. Mark Giordano
8. Key Arena
9. The Nashville Predators
10. 2021

Round 42 - St. Louis Blues
1. Dead last in the NHL.
2. Brett Hull, 86 goals.
3. Ryan O'Reilly
4. Brian Elliott
5. Erik Johnson
6. 4
7. Keith Tkachuk
8. Ryan O'Reilly
9. The Boston Bruins - Bonus: Torey Krug
10. Alex Pietrangelo

Round 43 - Tampa Bay Lightning
1. Ross Colton
2. Ben Bishop
3. Martin St. Louis, #26.
4. Steven Stamkos
5. The Philadelphia Flyers
Bonus: The Los Angeles Kings
6. ThunderBug
7. Corey Perry
8. Paul Ysebaert
9. Mark Recchi and Dave Anderychuk.
10. Victor Hedman

Round 44 - Toronto Maple Leafs
1. Tim Horton, he could lift a 40-gallon oil drum.
2. True
3. Darryl Sittler
4. Mats Sundin
5. Wendell Clark - Bonus: True, the correct spelling would be Leaves not Leafs.
6. Arenas and St. Pats.
7. 0
8. Auston Matthews
9. Dion Phaneuf
10. George Armstrong

Round 45 - Vancouver Canucks
1. Barry Wilkins
2. 3
3. Markus Naslund
4. Donald Brashear
5. Henrik Sedin
6. Henrik and Daniel Sedin.
7. Travis Konecny
8. Roger Neilson
9. Pavel Bure
10. Vasily Podkolzin

Round 46 - Vegas Golden Knights
1. 58, after the Vegas shooting.
2. David Perron
3. The Fortress
4. To pay homage to his Alma mater, the United States Military Academy.
5. Mark Stone
6. Marc-Andre Fleury and Robin Lehner.
7. William Karlsson
8. Cody Glass
9. Calvin Pickard
10. Nolan Patrick

Round 47 - Washington Capitals
1. Alexander Ovechkin
2. Rob Langway
3. Dynamo Moscow
4. Dale Hunter because he spent so much time in it.
5. Jay Beagle
Bonus: Idaho Steelheads, Hershey Bears, and Washington Capitals.
6. The Vegas Golden Knights
7. Alexander Ovechkin
8. 2013-2014
Bonus: Traktor Chelyabinsk
9. Mike Green
10. 3

Round 48 - Winnipeg Jets
1. Nikolaj Antropov
2. Mark Scheifele
3. Two, Blake Wheeler and Bryan Little.
4. Ondrej Pavelec
5. White
6. Manitoba Moose
7. Andrew Ladd and Blake Wheeler.
8. Ilya Kovalchuk
9. Bryan Little
10. University of Michigan
Bonus: Blake Wheeler, Bryan Little, Andrew Ladd, Evander Kane, Braydon Coburn, and Zach Bogosian.

Year	Matchup	Score	Winner
2002	Carolina Hurricanes	1-4	Detroit Red Wings
2003	Mighty Ducks of Anaheim	3-4	New Jersey Devils
2004	Calgary Flames	3-4	Tampa Bay Lightning
2006	Edmonton Oilers	3-4	Carolina Hurricanes
2007	Ottawa Senators	1-4	Anaheim Ducks
2008	Pittsburgh Penguins	2-4	Detroit Red Wings
2009	Detroit Red Wings	3-4	Pittsburgh Penguins
2010	Philadelphia Flyers	2-4	Chicago Blackhawks
2011	Vancouver Canucks	3-4	Boston Bruins
2012	New Jersey Devils	2-4	Los Angeles Kings
2013	Boston Bruins	2-4	Chicago Blackhawks
2014	New York Rangers	1-4	Los Angeles Kings
2015	Tampa Bay Lightning	2-4	Chicago Blackhawks
2016	San Jose Sharks	2-4	Pittsburgh Penguins
2017	Nashville Predators	2-4	Pittsburgh Penguins
2018	Vegas Golden Knights	1-4	Washington Capitals
2019	Boston Bruins	3-4	St. Louis Blues
2020	Dallas Stars	2-4	Tampa Bay Lightning
2021	Montreal Canadiens	1-4	Tampa Bay Lightning
2022	Tampa Bay Lightning	2-4	Colorado Avalanche

Round 50 - Opening Night & NHL Debuts

1. The Anaheim Ducks
2. The Ottawa Senators
3. 2012-2013 season and 2020-2021 season.
4. The Atlanta Flames and New York Islanders.
5. Kevin Stevens
6. The Ottawa Senators and the Toronto Maple Leafs. The Senators won.
7. The Colorado Avalanche
8. Troy Grosenick
9. Ryan Poehling
10. Derek Stepan
11. David Ayers
12. Scott Foster and he is an accountant.
13. Auston Matthews
14. Yes, because he registered time in an NHL game.
15. Kellan Lain
16. Josh Harding

Round 51 - Drafts of Famous Players
1. New York Islanders
2. Tampa Bay Lightning
3. Los Angeles Kings
4. Quebec Nordiques
5. Calgary Flames
6. Boston Bruins
7. Boston Bruins
8. Atlanta Thrashers
9. Chicago Blackhawks
10. Atlanta Thrashers
11. Ottawa Senators
12. Hartford Whalers
13. Boston Bruins
14. Ottawa Senators
15. Calgary Flames
16. San Jose Sharks
17. Minnesota North Stars
18. New York Islanders
19. New Jersey Devils
20. Boston Bruins

Round 52 - Olympic & World Cup Teams
1. Eric Staal
2. Andy Miele
3. Roberto Luongo
4. Ryan Miller
5. Zach Parise and Brian Rafalski
6. 1998
7. Sidney Crosby
8. Finland
9. Hayley Wickenheiser, Caroline Ouellette, Jayna Hefford
10. Canada finished in 3rd, winning Bronze. United States finished in 7th.
11. Canada and in Toronto, Ontario.
12. 1930s (1930)
13. Czech Republic
14. 27
15. 5
16. Tampere and Helsinki
17. Czechia
18. Vladislav Tretiak
19. 1960
20. Soviet Union

Round 53 - Minor League
1. The Adirondack Phantoms
2. The Hershey Bears
3. The Connecticut Whale
4. The Providence Reds
5. The Hershey Bears
6. The Chicago Wolves and the Grand Rapids Griffins.
7. Palm Springs, California.
8. The Colorado Eagles
9. The Henderson Silver Knights
10. Washington Capitals, Tampa Bay Lightning, Colorado Avalanche, Philadelphia Flyers, Boston Bruins, Quebec Nordiques, Buffalo Sabres, Pittsburgh Penguins, and Detroit Red Wings.
11. The Fort Wayne Komets
12. Les Cunningham Award
13. Atlantic Coast Hockey League and All-American Hockey League.
14. The West Coast Hockey League.
15. 2 Presidents Cups and 2 Kelly Cups.
16. Willie Marshall
17. Johnny Bower
18. Jonathan Quick
19. Brayden Holtby
20. The Last Vegas Wranglers

Round 54 - Hall of Fame
1. It was established in 1943.
2. 3 years
3. True
4. False, Gordie How and Guy Lafleur both did as well.
5. Bobby Orr
6. Dit Clapper
7. 9 straight years.
8. Anatoly Tarasov
9. In Old Toronto, Toronto, Ontario.
10. No, it is an independent organization.

11. The Bank of Montreal, it survived the Toronto fire of 1904.
12. True, it resides in the bank vault at the Hall of Fame.
13. 300 (294)
14. Yes, over 40.
15. Ontario
16. Temple de la renommée du hockey
17. Marián Hossa
18. True
19. False, there is 7 with the most recent being inducted in 2019.
Bonus: Manon Rheaume.
20. The Hockey Hall of Fame in Toronto.

Round 55 - NHL Draft Firsts
1. Nathan Walker
2. Leo Komarov
3. Rumun Ndur
4. George Geran
5. Anton and Peter Stastny
6. John Miszuk
7. Anze Kopitar
8. Yutaka Fukufuji
9. Craig Adams
10. Alexander Georgiev

Round 56 - NCAA Hockey
1. Michigan
2. 2
3. The semi-finals and finals of the college men's ice hockey tournament?
4. Big Ten
5. Peyton Jones
6. Owen Power
7. University of North Dakota
8. The award given to the top NCAA men's ice hockey player.
Bonus: An amateur hockey player who died in France during WW1.
9. The Calder Memorial Trophy.
10. Paul Kariya
11. Cole Caulfield
12. Minnesota-Duluth at 6.
13. The University of Denver
14. Annual tournament in Boston, Mass between Boston University, Boston College, Northwestern University and Harvard University.
15. Boston College

Round 57 - Arenas I

Arena	Capacity	Team
KeyBank Center	19,070	Buffalo Sabres
Bridgestone Arena	17,159	Nashville Predators
Crypto.com Arena	18,230	Los Angeles Kings
Canadian Tire Centre	19,347	Ottawa Senators
Rogers Place	18,347	Edmonton Oilers
Mullett Arena	4,600	Arizona Coyotes
PPG Paints Arena	18,387	Pittsburgh Penguins
Amalie Arena	19,092	Tampa Bay Lightning
Little Caesars Arena	19,515	Detroit Red Wings
Enterprise Center	18,096	St. Louis Blues
Xcel Energy Center	17,954	Minnesota Wild
United Center	19,717	Chicago Blackhawks
Madison Square Garden	18,006	New York Rangers
Scotiabank Saddledome	19,289	Calgary Flames
FLA Live Arena	19,250	Florida Panthers
UBS Arena	17,255	New York Islanders

Round 58 - Arenas II

Arena	Capacity	Team
Honda Center	17,174	Anaheim Ducks
Prudential Center	16,514	New Jersey Devils
Rogers Arena	18,910	Vancouver Canucks
SAP Center	17,562	San Jose Sharks
Capital One Arena	18,573	Washington Capitals
PNC Arena	18,680	Carolina Hurricanes
Ball Arena	17,809	Colorado Avalanche
Nationwide Arena	18,144	Columbus Blue Jackets
T-Mobile Arena	17,367	Vegas Golden Knights
American Airlines Center	18,532	Dallas Stars
Canada Life Centre	15,321	Winnipeg Jets
Scotiabank Arena	18,800	Toronto Maple Leafs
Bell Centre	21,105	Montreal Canadiens
TD Garden	17,565	Boston Bruins
Wells Fargo Center	19,538	Philadelphia Flyers
Climate Pledge Arena	17,151	Seattle Kraken

You have now come to the end of the quiz. I hope you have enjoyed the book and learnt many astonishing facts about the great game of hockey and NHL to impress your mates and family.

As a small independent publisher, positive reviews left on our books go a long way to attracting new readers who share your passion for the game.

If you are able to take a few minutes out of your day to leave a review it would be greatly appreciated!

If you find any issues you would like to raise, **please email me before leaving a negative review** with any comments you may have.

I will be more than happy to liaise with you and can offer refunds or updated copies if you are unhappy with your purchase.

Have a great day,

Marcus

marcustaylorpublications@yahoo.com

Made in the USA
Middletown, DE
07 May 2024

53981746R10057